TEN CAREFUL OWNERS

TEN CAREFUL
OWNERS

THE CARS THAT TIME FORGOT

STEVE SPELLER

INTRODUCTION

LEFT: 1960 Ford Popular interior. This all seems so spartan by today's standards.

LEFT: A Wolseley grill badge – it glows in the dark!

I didn't learn to drive until I was 36. We lived in London where the convenience of owning a car is outweighed by the inconvenience of actually driving it anywhere, besides which there's an extensive, though idiosyncratic, public transport system. For a long time, then, it seemed hardly worthwhile to bother learning. But when we decided to leave London it became a necessity.

We moved to Worthing, on the South coast, in 1998 and began to feel our way around in our newly-acquired car, savouring the comparatively open roads. During our early explorations I became aware of seemingly large numbers of old cars, mostly British, being driven about in what appeared to be daily use. This was something you generally didn't see in central London – cars just don't seem to last long in big cities, due probably to a lack of garage space and bad driving. I started to speculate on the cause of this apparently local

RIGHT: Beneath the
hood of a 1932
Singer Junior. Room
for so much more.

phenomenon. At first I put it down to the fact that the coast has traditionally been a retirement area. Perhaps it was simply lots of old people still driving around in the cars that they'd brought with them when they moved.

Whatever the reason, it was thrilling to spot these ageing vehicles, most of which I remembered from my childhood, still ambling along merrily at the turn of the century. It also dawned on me that most of the manufacturers of these cars were now long gone: here was a reminder of the British car industry's slow demise. What had been one of the world's biggest mass-producing industries 50 years ago was now a mere shadow of its former self. Austin, Morris,

Riley, Wolseley, Standard-Triumph, Hillman, Humber, Singer, Sunbeam – all were gone. These few cars were the last vestiges of that era, on their final fling before trading tarmac for museum or scrapyard.

ABOVE: The infamous "Quartick" steering wheel of a Mk1 Austin Allegro.

I decided to start documenting some of these cars and their owners (for what is a car without a driver?) before they disappeared, with a view to holding an exhibition of the photographs a couple of years later. It was not going to be about "classic" cars as such, but more about capturing a "living industrial archaeology". It was also important, where possible, to show these cars and people in everyday situations – like home or work – as opposed to setting them in scenic backgrounds and going for a glamorous angle.

At first I began leaving notes on the windscreens of vehicles that I came across… This resulted in a total of roughly one in every four owners getting in touch with me. Like most people, I suppose, if I find a note stuck to my windscreen I presume it's probably an offer to help me earn cash in my spare time while losing weight, so I screw it up and throw it away.

However, after a few months, the collection was gathering momentum and I felt comfortable enough to approach Worthing's Museum and Art Gallery to try and persuade them to let me have an exhibition. They liked the pictures, the collection dealt with a reasonably local topic, and, by coincidence, it tied in with another exhibition proposal based on the town's pavements, so they were quite happy to do it. Now I had a definite objective and schedule.

I decided to contact the local press. Articles about the project ran in both the Brighton Argus and the Worthing Herald, where they also appealed for owners of old cars to contact me if they wanted to participate in the project. Almost immediately, people all over began telephoning me to tell me about all manner of interesting vehicles. It was so wonderfully varied with everything from pristine classics to rough-and-ready work-a-day cars. Equally of interest were the owners, and it was through them that I began to get an insight into the world of old car ownership.

It was partly true about retired people still driving ageing British motors, though I didn't get to photograph many of these examples due mainly, I think, to a certain wariness in older owners at coming forward. It was also evident that many cars were in circulation due to elderly people "giving up" driving because of ill health or literally being scared off the road. One such example was a lovely old Riley 4/72 from the '60s which I found sitting in a quiet side street. Though still in a reasonable condition, it had very obviously not been driven

ABOVE: The 1966 Riley 4/72.

for some time and grass was beginning to grow around the wheels next to the kerb. Some time later the owner's son contacted me, having found one of my notes, and explained that his father had gone into a retirement home some months before. He asked me if I knew anyone who might be interested in buying it… Soon, it was gone.

A number of older motors were owned by young people for reasons ranging from the "cool" appeal to disdain for bland modern car design, or sometimes simply due to an interest in old cars that had passed from one generation to the next.

LEFT, ABOVE, RIGHT:
The Daimler,
Singer and Riley
badges of honour.

Familiarity was another factor. Some people had been driving the same car for decades. As long as it remained reasonably reliable, they felt at ease and had no desire for modern conveniences; and, as it was relatively cheap to run, they felt no compulsion to change.

Nostalgia plays a large role too. Some owners learned to drive in a certain model or passed their driving test in one, or a family member once owned the same car, and it brought back fond memories for them. In one street, quite close to where I live, the keeping and cherishing of old cars had almost become a craze, with no less than five out of about 60 homes owning old cars (including an ex-United Nations armoured car, which apparently was street-legal).

Something else, which puzzled me, was how people kept these cars running when spare parts were no longer manufactured. It seems that for every make – sometimes even for individual models – there is a club that you can join. If you need a certain part, by contacting the club, it can almost always be sourced. Failing that, people can be very resourceful by either improvising, making the part

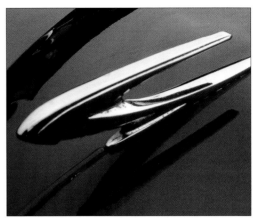

themselves or finding someone else who can do it. The Internet is also helpful, with sites dedicated to almost any car you can think of.

What will happen in the future? Though the numbers of these cars will gradually decrease, the enthusiasm for them will not. (In the years since I started, many of the cars I photographed have gone – though I still keep spotting fresh ones.) When you consider that the average life-span of a car is about 15 years, it's quite a feat to make one last for 40 years or more. It's great that people spend time and energy maintaining and driving them and deriving huge amounts of pleasure in the process. So, if you have the time, space and sufficient money, why not indulge yourself?

As a final word, I'd like to thank all the people in this book for giving a little bit of their time and sharing with me their part in our automotive history... and even occasionally letting me drive their cars!

ABOVE: The aerodynamic hood emblem of a Standard Vanguard.

STEVE SPELLER

1964 FORD ANGLIA 105E DELUXE

MR ALEXANDER

907cc 4 cylinder engine, 125,000+ genuine miles, never restored and all parts original,
bought from the first owner, an elderly gentlemen in Bournemouth, for £850.

*"I bought it for the styling more than anything. It's typically British for that period,
but with that American influence."*

1974 FORD ESCORT MK1 1100L
MR & MRS ANDERSON
1100cc 4 cylinder engine, 47,000+ miles, almost all parts original, completely restored,
owned since 2000, four previous owners.

"It's a very relaxed drive, driving as it used to be."
"Driving for pleasure, not in the fast lane."

1976 Austin Maxi 1750 Automatic
MR ARNOLD
1750cc 4 cylinder engine, 70,006 miles, all original parts, bought in 1999 from the original owner, who lived in Canada and only came back to drive it about two months a year.

"We bought it mainly for its scarcity."

1967 TRIUMPH HERALD 13/60 CONVERTIBLE
MRS BALL
1300cc 4 cylinder engine, 115,000 miles, bonnet from a Triumph Vitesse, owned since September 2000, bought locally from owners who'd had it for 15 years.

"We both enjoy classics, and we wanted something the children could join in with and have fun in."

1978 FORD ESCORT MK2 1.3L
MR BARTLETT
1300cc 4 cylinder engine, 24,428 miles, owned from new and bought in Twickenham, all original parts.

"The fella who sold me it said, 'It'll see you out.' Well I'm still here."

1976 VAUXHALL VIVA
MRS BEAUMONT
1300cc 4 cylinder engine, 31,676 miles, all original parts including tyres, bought in 2000 from the original lady owner, who was going into a retirement home.

"It was an absolute bargain, but I'd rather have a new car."

1955 JAGUAR XK140 SE
MR BONE
3400cc straight 6 cylinder engine, 37,000+ miles (not verified), refurbished between 1988–91 for rallying, and owned since 1999, exchanged for an E-Type.

"I love cars from the '30s and '40s and the XK140 is, in my opinion, the prettiest of the Jags."

1971 ROVER P6 2000TC & 1960 FORD PREFECT 107E
MS BOULTER

P6 – 2000cc engine, twin carbs, 86,181 miles, all parts original, owned since 1995,
used for everyday driving. Prefect – 997cc 4 cylinder OHV engine, 138,900+ miles,
mostly original parts, the car in which she learned to drive and passed her test, owned since 1981.

"I just prefer older cars. I owned a VW Golf for a while and absolutely hated it."

1962 VAUXHALL CRESTA PA
MR BOXALL

2600cc straight 6 cylinder engine, 57,000+ genuine miles, bought as a body shell and rear axle in 1999 and rebuilt from parts and a donor-vehicle from Liverpool.

"It was about the closest any British company got to a really American style."

1960 ALVIS TD21 SALOON
MS BYFORD
3000cc straight 6 cylinder engine, 100,000+ miles, owned since circa 1981, bought in Germany whilst in the army, several previous owners.

"I was drawn to it when I first saw it, and it gives me a great buzz to drive."

1977 AUSTIN ALLEGRO 1300 AUTOMATIC
MR CALLAN

1300cc 4 cylinder engine, 39,608 genuine miles, all parts original, but the previous original owner installed wooden fascia, clock and cassette, owned since 1988.

"It was pristine when we bought it in 1988, having done 6,000 miles in its first 11 years."

1937 MORRIS EIGHT SERIES 2 SALOON
MR CROWHURST
8hp 4 cylinder engine, mileage unknown, mostly original parts, garaged for 20 years until purchased in October 2000.

"Heritage, tradition and nostalgia."

1979 AUSTIN PRINCESS 2.2 HL AUTOMATIC
MR & MRS DEAN
2200cc 6 cylinder engine, 25,367 miles, all parts original except rear seat-belts,
owned since 2001, only one previous owner.

"It was the condition of it that won me over. It was absolutely spotless."

1971 TRIUMPH 2000 MK2 AUTOMATIC
MR DELAMARE
2000cc straight 6 cylinder engine, 60,485 genuine miles, all original parts, owned since 2000,
only one previous owner.

"It's a different world driving this to a modern car."

1970 E-TYPE JAGUAR
MR DIPROSE

4200cc straight 6 cylinder engine, 45,176 miles, mostly original parts.

"Granddad's bit of pleasure – I like to pose in it."

1952 STANDARD VANGUARD MODEL 1A
MR DOVE
2088cc 4 cylinder engine, 24,500+ genuine miles, all original parts and thoroughly restored,
owned since 1999.

"I bought it for sentimental reasons. I drove one in the army."

1952 HUMBER SUPER SNIPE MK3

MR EASTON

4000cc straight 6 cylinder engine, 145,000+ genuine miles, never restored, owned since 1956, originally owned by a former Lord Mayor of Hastings.

"In 1956 I had a Vauxhall 12 and I wanted a Cresta, but I ended up buying this Humber."

1975 MINI CLUBMAN ESTATE
MR ELLIS
998cc 4 cylinder engine, 75,000+ miles, all original parts and owned from new.

"It's always been reliable – I can't criticise it."

1975 HILLMAN HUNTER
MR NIKKHAH–ESHGHI
1725cc 4 cylinder engine, 64,000+ miles, all original parts and owned since 1995.

*"The presses for the Hunter were sold to Iran when it ceased production in Britain.
It was one of the first cars I drove as a young man."*

1955 STANDARD EIGHT
MR FAUL

1000cc 4 cylinder engine, 110,000+ miles, mostly original parts, except engine (from a Triumph Herald), but re-sprayed, bought in 1965 for £90.

"I have more fun driving this than I do modern cars."

1978 VAUXHALL VIVA 1300 GLS
MS FEDAK

1300cc 4 cylinder engine, 49,000+ genuine miles, all original parts, one previous owner who'd gone into a rest home, owned since 2001, bought to replace a 1974 Viva, which she'd driven for 14 years.

"It makes me feel very individual. People know me by my car."

1973 ROVER P5B COUPE 3.5 V8 AUTO
MR FERRIS
3500cc V8 engine, 90,000+ miles, all parts are original but re-sprayed,
owned since August 2000.

"I just love old British cars. I've belonged to the SD1 and Jaguar club."

1967 DAIMLER 2.5L
MR FORREST

V8 engine, 130,000 miles, engine re-conditioned, body re-sprayed, owned since new.

"Compared to modern Daimlers and Jaguars, this has quality and individuality".

1978 ROLLS ROYCE SILVER SHADOW MK2
MR GIBBINS
6750cc V8 engine, 28,000+ miles, all completely original, owned since 1994.

"It's the ultimate driving experience. Then there's the pride in driving something which is so typically British."

1973 TRIUMPH TOLEDO 1300
MS GOMEZ
1300cc 4 cylinder engine, 31,674 genuine miles, all original parts (even the brochure!),
owned since 1996.

"I inherited it from an aunt who gave up driving in her 80s."

1961 MORRIS 1000 TRAVELLER
MR GRAHAM
998cc 4 cylinder engine, 98,000+ miles, mostly original parts but new gearbox, re-conditioned engine, modernised electrics, used since August 2000.

"It's not actually mine. I'm selling it on behalf of my sister-in-law who's emigrated to Australia."

1964 ROVER 110
MR GRANT
2600cc 6 cylinder engine, 43,000+ miles but could be 100,000 or 200,000 more, most parts original, bought in 1993 in Arundel for £800.

"It's indulgence and escapism. I learned to drive in one."

1971 LOTUS ELAN +2 130S
MR GRIFFIN
1500cc 4 cylinder engine, twin carbs, all parts original but engine re-built, owned since 1998, exchanged for a diamond ring.

"Of all the numerous cars I own, it's my favourite."

1947 JAGUAR MK4 1.5L

MR HALL

1500cc 4 cylinder engine, mileage unknown, mostly original parts, refurbished over two years
following purchase in 1998, various owners, first owner from Barrow-in-Furness.

"I feel a real sadness at the demise of the British car industry."

1974 MGB GT

MR HALL

1800cc 4 cylinder engine, mileage unknown, mostly original parts, engine and gearbox re-conditioned, owned since 1987.

"It's a joy to drive. I use it almost every day."

1960 FORD POPULAR
MS HALLSWORTH

1172cc 4 cylinder engine, 116,927 miles, restored late '90s, three previous owners, of which the second and third were father and son in Lancashire, bought at auction in Huntingdon in August 2001.

"It was complete happenstance. I wanted a classic, something robust and maintainable, and I liked the idea of sustainability and recycling."

1962 HUMBER HAWK (SERIES 2)
MR HARMAN
2200cc 4 cylinder engine, 61,036 genuine miles, bought in 1975 for £145, two previous owners, originally registered in Hampton Court, London.

"I've been driving Humbers since 1968. They're very comfortable and roomy."

1929 AUSTIN 7 'TOP HAT' RK SALOON
MR & MRS HAYES

7hp 4 cylinder side-valve engine, true mileage unknown, most parts original, owned since 1998, previously stored in a garage for 25 years as part of a private collection.

"We had an Austin 7 when we just married in 1954. They're easy to maintain and the club is very friendly."

1931 MORRIS MINOR 2 SEATER 'SPORTS'
MR HEASMAN
885cc 4 cylinder side-valve engine, true mileage unknown, all parts original except modifications to brakes and shock absorbers, owned since 1999.

"Love at first sight!"

1975 RELIANT SCIMITAR GTE
MS HENDERSON
3000cc V6 engine, 118,861 genuine miles, most parts original including re-conditioned engine,
owned since 1978.

*"We wanted something that would last, wouldn't rust, and was fast and looked good.
When we realised that they were no longer making them it seemed even more attractive."*

1970 FORD ESCORT MK1 1300
MR HERRIDGE
1300cc 4 cylinder engine, 23,000+ miles (though more likely 123,000), mostly original parts but not the engine, re-sprayed.

"I prefer and have owned American classics, but this is a great little runaround."

1973 FORD ESCORT MK1 1300 AUTOMATIC
MR HOAR
1300cc 4 cylinder engine, 33,000+ genuine miles, all original parts, owned since 1999.

"It belonged to my daughter-in-law's grandmother. I was going to sell it but I've grown quite attached to it."

1981 AUSTIN ALLEGRO 1300
MRS HOSIER
1300cc 4 cylinder engine, 30,000+ miles, all original parts except clutch, owned since 1995.

"It's a car with a soul. You feel it has a character... You can talk to it!"

1948 LEA FRANCIS 14HP 4-LIGHT SALOON & 1948 14HP 2-SEATER SPORTS
MR JENKINS

Sports – 1746cc 4 cylinder OHC engine, mileage unknown, most parts original, bought in parts in 1999. Saloon – 1748cc 4 cylinder engine, 88,821 miles, bought in 1995 in York, restored in 1998, several previous owners.

"I owned a Lea Francis Saloon in the '60s and, when I retired, I bought another one, but then I realised I'd have more fun with a sports car. So I bought this and restored it."

1965 SINGER GAZELLE
MR JOHNSON
1725cc 4 cylinder engine, 51,850 miles, all parts original. Owned since 2000, possibly only the second owner.

"They attract an awful lot of attention. People like them, they're friendly."

1957 AUSTIN JB107 AMBULANCE
MR JONES
1500cc 4 cylinder BMC B series engine, mileage unknown, all original parts, owned since 1980
and previously owned by his father for 8–9 years.

"You can do everything you need to in it and it's pretty!"

1968 RILEY ELF AUTOMATIC
MR JONES
998cc 4 cylinder engine, mileage unknown, most parts original, owned since 1991.

"I bought Elf in 1991 because it made me smile when I looked at it."

1965 MORRIS MINI MINOR 850 DELUXE
MR KELLEWAY

850cc 4 cylinder engine, true mileage unknown, owned since 2000, all parts original, except brakes, and re-sprayed, having spent 22 years stored away in a garage.

"I've always been into Minis and I saw this as a challenge."

1956 MORRIS MINOR SERIES 2
MR KETT
803cc 4 cylinder OHV engine (original!), 46,427 genuine miles, bought locally from a newspaper advert from the only original owner in July 1999.

"It's very easy to drive. With a bigger car I'd need power-steering."

1981 TRIUMPH DOLOMITE 1500
MR KINGS
1500cc 4 cylinder engine, 52,600+ miles, all original parts, only two previous owners.

"It was my son's, but he never used it, so he gave it to me."

1965 AUSTIN A35 VAN AV8
MR LAWRENCE
1098cc 4 cylinder engine, 64,000+ genuine miles, all original parts, originally owned by the army, based in Germany, bought in Bedford in 2000 for £2,100.

"I owned the Countryman version back in 1969."

1964 VAUXHALL VIVA HA
MR LAWRENCE

1056cc 4 cylinder engine, 49,000+ miles, new carburettor, wing mirrors and minor paintwork, bought in 1993 for £650 in Brixham, Devon from the original owner.

"I'm re-living my youth. I passed my driving test in one at 17."

1966 MGB GT
MR LAWRENCE
1800cc 4 cylinder engine, 34,000+ miles on re-conditioned engine, owned since 1999,
re-sprayed to the original colour (the previous owner had sprayed it gold!).

"It's genetic!"

1966 HUMBER IMPERIAL
MR LEWIS
3000cc straight 6 cylinder engine, 49,000+ miles, all original parts, re-sprayed 1986, owned since 1997, originally owned by a millionaire businessman from Westcliff-on-Sea, Essex.

"I was already interested in old cars and then became infatuated with Humbers. This is my eighth."

1931 FORD MODEL A
MR LIDBETTER

24hp 4 cylinder engine (previously 14.9hp), 64,000+ genuine miles, unrestored except paintwork,
built in Manchester and originally sold in Lewes, East Sussex, bought for £7,500 in 1993,
only two previous owners.

"I've wanted one since I was in my 20s."

1963 WOLSELEY 16/60 AUTOMATIC
MR McCABE

1622cc 4 cylinder engine, 40,700 miles, all parts original but re-sprayed, owned since 2000, having spent 20 years untouched in a garage.

"The styling, more than anything, was what attracted me. That and the fact that it was an automatic."

1973 FORD CAPRI MK1 3000 V6 GT
MR MERRITT
3000cc V6 engine, 119,979 miles, all original parts, owned since 1997, bought in Southampton for £1,200 from the second owner.

"They're very individual cars. A very strong and influential design. This one also has a great sound."

1976 MINI CLUBMAN
MS MINCHIN
850cc 4 cylinder engine, 34,000+genuine miles, all original parts except carpets and speedo cable, owned since 1997, two previous owners.

"It was in really good condition and had a really low mileage for its year."

1952 JOWETT JUPITER MK1
MR NANKIVELL
1500cc Flat 4 cylinder engine, re-conditioned and not original, total restoration after buying it in bits in 1991, previous owner got it back on the road in 1972.

"When I bought my first Jowett the man that sold it to me said, 'Be careful, they're addictive.' He was absolutely right."

1967 JAGUAR MK2 3.4L
MS PATRICK
3400cc V6 engine, 56,000 miles (but could be 156,000), owned since September 2000

"We had one before, 14 years ago, and we seem to get drawn back to them."

1932 SINGER JUNIOR
MR PEGRAM

850cc 4 cylinder 7.8hp engine, true mileage unknown, owned since 2000 and rebuilt,
80% of the parts bought, only 200 examples of 25,000 models built 1927–32.

"I needed a project to keep me occupied. 2,000 parts and 1,000 hours later, here it is!"

1946 MORRIS EIGHT Z POST OFFICE TELEPHONE ENGINEERS VAN
MR PLANT
799cc 4 cylinder engine, true mileage unknown, owned since 1977, bought in Dorking for £60
from a builder who used it as his work van.

"There used to be thousands of these around once, but now there are only about nine left."

1963 FORD CONSUL CORTINA MK1 GT
MR PLANT
1500cc 4 cylinder engine, 60,418 miles, owned since beginning of 2000, all parts original.

"It was in really great condition after being forgotten about in a garage in Fittleworth for 13 years."

1972 SUNBEAM ALPINE COUPE
MR POSTLETHWAITE
1725cc 4 cylinder engine, 70,000+ miles, all original parts, bought in 1989 after part-exchanging a Mk3 Cortina plus £500.

"I love this car! It's easy to drive and comfortable."

1954 MG TF 1500
MR & MRS RISHBETH
1500cc 4 cylinder engine, mileage unknown, all parts are original, rebuilt in 1994 and owned since 1999.

"I always wanted one and was finally given permission."

1963 AUSTIN A60 PICKUP
MR SHARP
1600cc 4 cylinder B Series engine, 45,000+ miles, mostly original parts, but original colour was teal blue, bought in 2002 for £1,200, originally owned by Welsh hill farmers.

"I was looking for a Morris Minor Pickup and found this, which seemed somehow nicer."

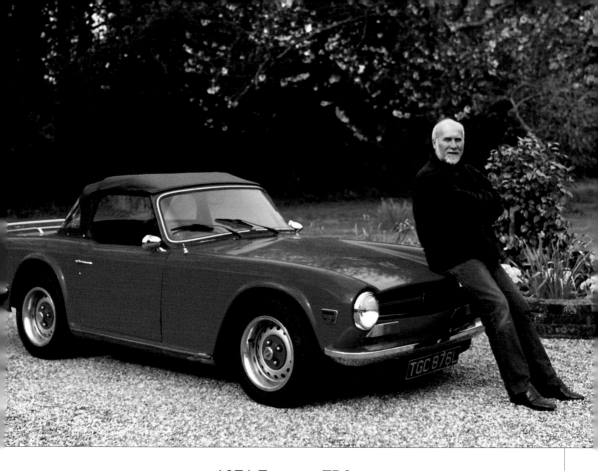

1971 TRIUMPH TR6

MR SHEARS

2500cc straight 6 cylinder injection engine, 63,000+ genuine miles, all original parts but re-sprayed (was pale yellow), owned since 1999.

"It reminds me of when I was 26 and it's almost the same car."

1967 RILEY KESTREL 1300
MISS SMITH
1275cc 4 cylinder engine, 141,000+ genuine miles, only one previous owner up to 1970.

"My brothers had very flashy cars like Bentleys. I thought I should drive something a little less affluent-looking."

1934 Vauxhall ASY Series 12 Light 6 Deluxe Saloon
MR SPENCER

12hp 4 cylinder engine, mileage unknown, mostly original parts, owned since 1966, said to have been owned by Lady Diana Cooper during World War Two.

"I acquired it from my grandmother in 1966."

AUSTIN ALLEGRO (VARIOUS)
MR SPENCER

Owns seven Allegros including three Series 2s, 2 Vanden Plas versions, a Mk3 and a Mk1
with the infamous "Quartick" steering wheel, all in running order.

"I was looking for a Mini when I spotted my first Allegro and it just took my fancy."

1960 WOLSELEY 1500 MK1
MR SPOONER
1489cc 4 cylinder engine, 60,388 miles, owned since 1984, bought for £169 and completely restored.

"We rescued it from a scrapyard in Lancing."

1954 RILEY 1.5L RME
MR SPOONER
1496cc 4 cylinder engine, true mileage unknown, bought in 1978 in Gloucester and totally restored between 1984–1988.

"It really is a pleasure to drive. It's like going back in time."

1966 HILLMAN MINX DELUXE
MS STALLARD
1725cc 4 cylinder engine, 107,978 miles, all parts original but re-sprayed in the '80s.

"It was bought new by my Grandfather from Caffyns and then passed to me in 1989."

1960 Austin Healey 'Frog eye' Sprite
MR STRACHAN
948cc 4 cylinder engine, 81,000+ miles, bought in Preston in 1991 for £6,500, nine previous owners.

"It's a lot of fun to drive and people relate to it."

1973 TRIUMPH SPITFIRE 4
MS SWIFT
1298cc 4 cylinder engine, 92,000+ miles, mostly original parts, owned since 1999,
several previous owners.

"I owned a blue one when I was younger."

1958 MG ZB MAGNETTE
MR TAPPENDEN
1489cc 4 cylinder OHV engine, owned since 1988, two previous owners, first owners were Denney Bros. (Bakeries) in Burnham, Buckinghamshire.

"It was one of a number of old cars that were found in a basement garage in a block in Hove, and I liked the look of it."

1969 BEDFORD CA CAMPERVAN
MR TEE

1750cc 4 cylinder engine, 82,050 miles (though it could be 182,050 miles), owned since 1995,
had not been driven since 1998.

"I paid £50 for it from a bloke in Portslade."

1963 MORRIS 1100
MS TOOGOOD
1100cc 4 cylinder engine, 46,006 genuine miles, all original parts and never restored, even the tyres were original when bought in 1992 in Ashtead, near Epsom, for £700 from its original owner.

"The previous owner's daughter wanted someone who'd run it and look after it. So I did."

1967 TRIUMPH HERALD 1200 CONVERTIBLE
MS TYLER
1200cc 4 cylinder engine, mileage unknown, owned since 1999.

"It was a present."

1971 ROVER P6 3500S
MR VASSIE
3500cc V8 engine, 67,160 miles, left-hand drive for U.S. market where it was owned by a British
Diplomat, complete restoration since purchase in 1997.

"I just love them and, besides, I restore them for a living."

1960 MORRIS OXFORD MK4
MR WARREN
1700cc 4 cylinder engine, 98,673 genuine miles, all original parts, owned since 1998,
bought locally for £900, various previous owners.

"When you drive around in a car like this it accrues interest from passers-by."

1961 AUSTIN A40 DELUXE
MR WEBB
904cc 4 cylinder OHV engine, 36,358 genuine miles, owned since 1991, originally registered in London.

"It was one of the first truly modern British cars, where they moved away from those post-war blobby shapes."

1976 TRIUMPH DOLOMITE 1500 HL
MR & MRS WILLIAMS
1500cc 4 cylinder engine, 105,000+ miles, only the second owners since 1983,
all parts original, but engine re-conditioned, re-sprayed in 1994.

"We like it and it's what we're used to."

1968 HILLMAN IMP CALIFORNIAN
MS WILLIAMS
850cc 4 cylinder rear engine, 113,982 miles, most parts original except engine, owned since 1980, bought for £220 from original owner.

"I love my Hillman. I've been offered new cars, but I've always refused."

1980 TRIUMPH DOLOMITE 1300
MR WILSON

1300cc 4 cylinder engine, 55,850 genuine miles, all original parts and only one set of tyres in 20 years, owned since 1981, one previous owner.

"We only use it about once a week now for shopping."

1978 Morris Marina 1.3 Super
MR WILSON
1300 4 cylinder engine, 30,000+ miles, owned from new and bought in Enfield, London,
all parts original (including two of the tyres) except two new front wings.

"We were thinking of buying an Escort, but decided on this instead."

1967 MORRIS MINOR CONVERTIBLE
MS WRIGHT
998cc 4 cylinder engine, 34,000+ genuine miles, all parts original except soft top, originally owned by her mother from new.

"It's always been in our family."

ACKNOWLEDGEMENTS

*Thank you to Alison Milner and Miriam Reik for help and encouragement;
Fred Stanford at Southern Classics for spreading the word.*

1973 Ford Capri Mk1 interior. The overzealous use of leatherette gives a certain classiness, but it must have been hell in hot weather.

First published in 2004 by
New Holland Publishers (UK) Ltd
London • Cape Town • Sydney • Auckland
www.newhollandpublishers.com

Garfield House
86–88 Edgware Road
London W2 2EA
United Kingdom

80 McKenzie Street
Cape Town 8001
South Africa

14 Aquatic Drive
Frenchs Forest
NSW 2086
Australia

218 Lake Road
Northcote, Auckland
New Zealand

2 4 6 8 10 9 7 5 3 1

ISBN 1 84330 904 1

Editor: Gareth Jones
Editorial Direction: Rosemary Wilkinson
Production Controller: Hazel Kirkman
Designer: Bill Mason
Photographer: Steve Speller

Reproduction by Modern Age Repro, Hong Kong
Printed and bound by Craft Print International, Singapore

Steve, Emma, Andy, Sindy and 188 ACD, circa 1969.